Jerry Pethick

Material Space

OCTOBER 19 – NOVEMBER 27, 1991

Southern Alberta Art Gallery

Southern Alberta Art Gallery

Jerry Pethick: Material Space

October 19 to November 27, 1991

Staff

Joan Stebbins: Director/Curator

Janet Walters: Administrative/Curatorial Assistant

David Wagner: Curatorial Intern

Lori Marquardson: Education/ Extension Officer

Daniel Smith: Gallery Technician/Registrar

Mike Murphy: Public Program Coordinator

David Clearwater: Weekend Attendant/Librarian

Design: Charles Cousins

Photography: Daniel Smith and Peter Green (Installation)

Colour Separation: Colour Four

Film Output: Paperwords

Printing: Paperworks Press Limited

Organized by the Southern Alberta Art Gallery with the assistance of The Canada Council

Jerry Pethick's work is represented by Galerie Brenda Wallace, Montreal and Cliff Michel Gallery, Seattle.

© 1992

Southern Alberta Art Gallery

601-3rd Avenue South

Lethbridge, Alberta

T1J 0H4

isbn: 0-921613-31-8

Front Cover:

Snake Deletion, Haystack and Sunrise (detail),1991

Photograph: Daniel Smith

Back Cover:

Colossus of Kindergarten, 1987/89

Photograph: Daniel Smith

Jerry Pethick: Bobsled, *1989 (left)*; Waterworks Park, *1972 (right)*

ACKNOWLEDGEMENTS

On behalf of the Southern Alberta Art Gallery I would like to thank the many people who contributed to the successful outcome of this endeavour. Jerry Pethick's work is all too little known in his own country and we were pleased to undertake a project which would attempt to change that. I would like to particularly thank the artist for his unwavering faith in our ability to meet the challenges of his work. His advice, assistance and good company throughout our collaboration ensured the success of this venture. During the installation we were offered assistance by others who believe in the artist's work. Our thanks go to Margaret Pethick, Lyle Chambers and Michael Hornsby for their long hours of patient help.

Jack Jeffrey encouraged me to pursue this exhibition and I am grateful for his insight. Cliff Michel in Seattle offered his enthusiastic support and Brenda Wallace in Montreal assisted through sponsoring a concurrent show of the artist's sculpture. We were fortunate to obtain the services of two writers who have followed Pethick's production over many years: Matthew Kangas in Seattle whose essay situates the work historically, and Annette Hurtig in Toronto who has spent many summers near the artist on Hornby Island. We are most grateful for their invaluable assessments of Jerry Pethick's art.

The production of this publication was ably managed by Charles Cousins in Calgary. We were pleased to be able to utilize the photographic skills of Daniel Smith and Peter Green of Lethbridge to document work in the exhibition and thank them for their contribution. Finally we are indebted to The Canada Council Exhibition Assistance Program which makes it possible for us to fulfill our mandate to present and document the work of Canadian artists.

5

Joan Stebbins
Director/Curator

Fig. 1

Fly's eye camera

made by

Jerry Pethick,

1987

Courtesy

of the artist

Material

PETHICK: Space

BY: MATTHEW KANGAS

INTRODUCTION

The role of the 20th–century artist has often been cast in that of differing identities. Marcel Duchamp and Marcel Broodthaers were *bricoleurs,* playful magicians making art appear and disappear at will. Salvador Dali and Andy Warhol were clowns and society courtiers, as eager to appall as to please patrons. Jerry Pethick could be seen as an inventor. Obsessed by the history of optical perception, the photograph, and the development of sculpture's potential, he has invented different kinds of sculpture which must be seen in the context of scientific developments since 1826 (the invention of photography) in order to be fully understood.

That Pethick's sculpture can be experienced and enjoyed without this understanding of scientific developments is entirely possible and a tribute to the artist's consummate control over materials. But when viewed in the long shadow of the developments of 19th–century optics, its meaning emerges. Just as the Impressionists and Post–Impressionists' awareness of photography permanently altered the way they painted, so his overriding interest in these issues and their relation to the optical perception of the three–dimensional object has changed his own art.

BACKGROUND

Born Gerald Thomas Bern Pethick in London, Ontario in 1935, he is the son of a man of many parts as well, a crane builder, carpenter, and tinsmith. As a young man, he worked side by side with Finnish–Canadian miners in the nickel mines of Ontario and marvelled at their mastery over tools and their ability to fashion materials to fit precisely into spaces without measuring in advance.

An early experience deep in the mines set the stage for the artist's curiosity about the flexible nature of light, sound, and space. Chosen to set the explosive charges once the holes are drilled, he was smoking a cigarette at the moment he pressed the detonator. As he watched the curling trail of cigarette smoke, everything shifted sideways in layers during the shuddering explosion. As the dust cleared seconds later, Pethick observed how the cigarette smoke, too, shifted back to exactly the same continuous configuration as if the charges had never happened. Chaos, pattern, and materials seemed closer together than he had ever imagined.

Going on to art school in England in 1957, he studied sculpture at the Chelsea Polytechnic in London with the Dame Elisabeth Frink and Bernard Meadows, later named head of Royal College of Art. After graduating from Chelsea with a National Diploma of Design, he set up his own studio, worked on waxes for bronzecasting, and met other artists from Commonwealth nations, like painter Frank Bowling of Guyana. Active in the Artists International Association and the Young Commonwealth Artists Group, he participated in their group shows and generally enjoyed life in what was soon to become "swinging London".

When Meadows offered Pethick a scholarship to attend the Royal College of Art, he readily accepted and entered into one of RCA's most fertile and exciting periods, 1961–64. Frink was again a teacher, along with Robert Clatworthy, George Fullard, Michael Kuellman (a former student of Cambridge philosopher Ludwig Wittgenstein) and critic John Berger. Fellow students included Roland Piche, Patrick Caulfield, Nigel Slight, and Allan Jones.

While still a student at the RCA, he heard a young rock 'n roll group, The Rolling Stones, play at a college dance.

It was in the years after the Royal College, 1964–67, that Pethick began to be seriously interested in technology and its application to sculpture. An international plastics exhibition held at Olympia Conference Centre in London in 1965 had an important impact and, before long, he had acquired vacuum–forming equipment, was experimenting with polyethylene, and using hot–air welding tools to bend plastic. To earn a living, he got a job as an art mover and gallery assistant with dealer Victor Waddington.

When Pethick called scientist Dennis Gabor of the Imperial College on the telephone in 1967, he wanted to learn more about Gabor's experiments with three–dimensional images, called holo-grams. "Maybe you've made sculpture obsolete!", Pethick recalls telling Gabor. "I hope so!", Gabor responded.

Thus ensued a long period of absorption in holograms which took him to New York; Ann Arbor, Michigan; San Francisco; Los Angeles; and back to London. Still immersed in the London art scene, he met and became friends with the painter

Fig. 3. World's

first photograph.

Nicephore Niepce:

View from

Window at Gras,

1826. Courtesy of

Gernsheim

Collection, Harry

Ranson Humanities

Research Center,

the University of

Texas at Austin.

Francis Bacon; playwright Tom Stoppard; American photo-realist Richard Haas; R. B. Kitaj; David Hockney and others.

It was another scientist at Imperial College, George Jull, who welcomed Pethick's interest in the three-dimensional photo process and suggested he meet Bell Laboratories' Robert Pole, as well as Roger de Montebello, researcher of integrams. He also met a laser physicist, Lloyd Cross of the Detroit defense contractor, KMS Industries. It was during this period, 1964–67, that he was first introduced to rolux, a lenticular sheeting material which is laminated together to create optical distortion. He made a series of drawings using rolux.

With Cross moving to London on business, Pethick's interest shifted to holography. Cross had brought to Britain a small laser. Pethick's small studio on Walmer Road in the Ladbroke Grove area was set up for laserwork with the idea of making his first holograms.

Combining Ilford spectroscopic plates, chemicals, and front-surface mirrors, Pethick repeatedly exposed plates with the laser. The subject, a real prawn on a white plastic X, was difficult but eventually a holographic image was captured. All of his heroes—photography inventor Nicephore Niepce (fig.3); theorist and painter Georges Seurat; and colour photography inventor Gabriel Lippmann (fig.4)—would have been proud. He had carried their experiments to the next logical step: space.

The following year, Pethick helped organize and was included in the first known holography exhibition at the Cranbrook Academy of Art gallery in Bloomfield Hills, Michigan. One year later, 1969, he was featured in the first holography show in New York, "N Dimensional Space" at the Finch College Museum of

Art and his work was warmly praised by *Newsweek* art critic Douglas Davis.

After living briefly in Ann Arbor and New York, Pethick settled in San Francisco in 1970. For the next five years until his return to Canada, he pursued a highly fruitful path of teaching, experimentation, and exploration of holograms leading to what he called "integral photography".

As a co-founder in 1971 of the first School of Holography in San Francisco, Pethick oversaw and taught classes which originally consisted of four classes of ten students each. Five major educational institutions in the Bay Area, including the University of California at Berkeley and the San Francisco Art Institute (where he had taught earlier), all agreed to offer academic credit for their students attending School of Holography classes. Several students became class assistants and two, Fred Unterseher and Lon Moore, went on to become well-known authorities on holography.

Pethick took full advantage of the available advanced technology in the Bay Area and experimented with many different lenses from the Optic Science Group, Inc., in San Rafael, California. For his first "integral photo", he took 256 2 ¼-by-2 ¼-inch photographs with Charles Frizzel of nearby Mt. Tamalpais using a Hasselblad camera. He shot through a large gridded sheet of plate glass held in a wooden frame, attempting to approximate a fly's-eye lens.

After processing 25 rolls of colour film, he placed the uncut 2 ¼-inch slides on a large sheet of plastic in rows, slightly altering the intervening spaces between each photograph. These were, in turn, sandwiched between two plastic sheets. A third sheet, held

Fig. 4. Gabriel

Lippmann in his

laboratory at the

Sorbonne, Paris,

1894 (note

stereoscopic camera

at right). Courtesy

of Jerry Pethick

Fig. 5. Jerry

Pethick: (detail)

Subject and

Object, 1990.

22 photos,

Fresnel lenses,

glass, rubber,

silicone, mixed

media. Courtesy of

the artist

away from the image with spacers, provided the surface for the lenses (fig. 5). Pethick placed one plastic lens over each image. Thus, when the viewer looks through first one lens and, then, two at once, a binocular or stereoscopic image appears to the eye. Stepping back gradually, more and more lenses enter the viewer's field of vision so that, given a distance of five to ten to twenty feet, a large overall image appears to hover *between* the sheets' surface and the viewer's body. As Douglas Davis put it in his *Newsweek* review, "now he is planning exceptionally complex forms that will float in large 'real' scale, perhaps 3 feet by 4 feet before the eye. He is finding his way to a new aesthetic, an aesthetic that preaches solidity while it practices the immaterial and insubstantial: the impossible, in brief, made possible." This is the core and essence of Pethick's "material space" concept, a kind of home-made three-dimensional image, not a hologram, but a viewer-activated visual experience approximating three dimensions. His next task would be to combine the "integral photos" with adjacent sculptural elements to complicate the visual field even more. His mature phase as a sculptor would occur where his life began: in Canada.

DEVELOPMENT

Recycling was a way of life for Pethick when he moved to remote Hornby Island off the British Columbia coast in 1975, both as a settler and as an artist. It was the crucial influence on his first mature phase as a sculptor and one which continues to affect him to this day. Pethick drew from the cast-offs at the Hornby

Island Recycling Depot for his sculptural materials: porcelain-enamel appliances, tires, washing machine agitators and tubs.

In this way, Pethick combined low-technology materials with high-technology optics. During the mid–1970s, he had intensified his inventor's researches into the later developments of early photography. Whereas Nicephore Niepce created the first fixed photograph in 1826 and later collaborated with Daguerre whom he met through their common lensmaker, Chevalier, it was a Sorbonne scientist, Gabriel Lippmann, who developed a full–colour photography process in 1891, for which he was awarded a Nobel Prize.

Germane to Pethick's interests, Lippmann had hypoth-esized that an array of slightly altered images of the same scene would reconstruct itself into a single image with depth, as Douglas Davis described above. This was scientifically proven by a Russian researcher in 1931 and by Pethick's friend at Bell Labs, Robert Pole, in 1961. The implications of all these breakthroughs became significant for Pethick's art.

They proved that, as Pethick put it, "space is the most important part of sculpture and vision is not a hierarchical sense."

Working away in a succession of studios on Hornby Island and subsequently in Paris, London, and Montreal, he has been able to retain an open, improvisatory flair in the appearance of his finished sculptures. They appear as objects in the process of being invented, without beginning or end. This has confounded many viewers and critics, accustomed as many of us are to more conventionally completed-looking types of sculpture, but this raw and often slapdash look is crucial to conveying the quality of

Fig. 6. Jerry

Pethick: (detail)

Margaret and

Yana and the

Century Plant,

1972. Black-and-

white photograph

Courtesy of the

artist

Fig. 7. Jerry

Pethick: (detail)

Composite

Portrait, *1989*

Black and white

photograph

Courtesy of the

artist

open-ended laboratory experimentation, what Pethick titled his Vancouver Art Gallery exhibition, "Traces of Discovery."

Glass began to play an important role in his art once he moved to Hornby Island and especially after his first of three visits to Pilchuck Glass School in Stanwood, Washington where he was resident artist at the invitation of director Dale Chihuly. He had already met experimental filmmaker and glass artist Paul Marioni in 1974 during his San Francisco sojourn, but it was the availability of recycled glass such as light bulbs on Hornby Island and the possibility of having anything he wished made in glass at Pilchuck that freed up Pethick to use glass in accentuating its transparency, optical properties, and liquid qualities.

This material development coincided with his renewed and growing preoccupation with early 20th-century optics. He adapted Auguste Fresnel's invention of a flattened glass lens for use in lighthouses to his own "integral photos" and dedicated a piece to the Frenchman, *The Lighthouse Invites the Storm/Charting Undulation* (1982). Fresnel's lenses, now widely used in theatre lighting and often manufactured in plastic, compressed and intensifed light in the same way that Pethick wished to abruptly channel the way the viewer traditionally perceives an image. From 1986 on, the grid of Fresnel lenses placed a few inches over the rows of photo images would become a repeated, essential hallmark of his most ambitious sculptures.

Maturity

No one in the world is making sculptures quite like Jerry Pethick's. His particular concatenation of objects, perceptual goals, and historic allusions combine in an absolutely unique experience at once challenging, frustrating, and ultimately enjoyable and humourous. It has taken nearly 30 years to bring together all the diverse activities and the results are among the most intriguing artworks of the present decade. They combine an early-modernist preoccupation with the unreliable aspects of optical vision seen in the anti-realist representation of, say, Cubism or Futurism, and the distinctly postmodern concerns with what critic Rosalind Krauss called sculpture's "expanded field" of non-unified materials, placement, and ecological issues such as recycling.

At the same time, autobiography, psychology, and subjectivity also are significant aspects of Pethick's art. With the multipartite nature of a Pethick sculpture often confusing the viewer, he or she is thrown back on his or her own resources, forced to look inward for possible recognizable references drawn from prior experience, and gently led outward to confront the realization that the perception of the artwork is inextricably tied to the presence and physical position of the viewer's own body.

Terribly resistant to photographic reproduction, Pethick's art is itself a scientific and artistic conundrum. If the meaning of the work resides in the viewer's gradual awareness of his or her own relationship to the three-dimensional floating "material space", how could this internal, retinal phenomenon possibly be captured by a camera? Thus, the one contemporary artist most

Fig. 8. Jerry

Pethick: The

Seventh Screen/

Returning You

to Regular

Programming

(1984), enamel,

steel, mixed media,

58 by 106 by 2

in. City Light

1% Portable Works

Collection, Seattle

Arts Commission.

Acc. CL84.051.

obsessed by the implications of photography cannot fully benefit from photography's recording power of his achievements.

Given this caveat, we arrive at another facet of Pethick's contributions. He has returned the art experience to the individual viewer, taking it away from the pervasive mediations of technology in the form of the photographic art reproduction. To borrow the subtitle of his 1980 *Seventh Screen* (fig. 8), he is "returning you to regular programming", not the reassuring drone of passive television viewing but the unusual experience of seeing three-dimensional objects in a perspective relationship to a floating, stereoscopic image. Radically subversive in the sense that this makes us question profoundly what we think we are seeing the rest of the time, Pethick's 1960s sensibility has triumphed in the opposite, conformist and consumerist 1980s and 1990s. His art is both a tonic and a warning that we must question everything (beginning with empirical vision) as well as contemplate the results of a throwaway society.

The final years of the 1980s saw a succession of major sculptures which operate on a number of different levels: ecological, personal, perceptual, historical.

After exhibitions in Victoria, Vancouver, and Seattle, he proceeded to refine the dominant image in each tableau or installation into something more simplified and recognizable: a dog, a cat, a wheelbarrow, a treasure chest. These objects—often created out of accretive, repetitive materials like cardboard tubes or glass balls—became the foreground in the complicated experience of "material space". That is, when first encountering a double-part sculpture, i.e., floor object and wall-mounted integral photo, the floor object (dog, wheelbarrow, boat, etc.)

dominates our vision because of its size. Upon approaching and "locking into" the binocular image of the "integral photo", it enlarges as one steps backward from the wall. At a certain point, the floor object complicates the field of vision by acting as a second, intruding element. This real 3-D object echoes the "unreal" material space image in our eye and the experience of seeing both at the same time becomes our whole visual record of the work: figure and ground are merged into one view.

All of this is tied to Pethick's early interchange with Dennis Gabor about the advent of holography making sculpture "obsolete". Far from rendering sculpture obsolete, in his hands, the implications of manufactured, evanescent three–dimensional images led to an art which simulates the electronic event of holography. Instead of a machine, he has conceived of ways for the unaided human eye to accomplish the same thing. Maybe it is Pethick who now deserves the Nobel Prize—or at the very least an O.B.E.

DISMANTLING PETHICK

The temptation with Pethick is to discuss, as most commentators have, the context for his sculptures, their allusions to scientific history, for example, instead of their formal properties and attendant meaning. In this essay, I share some of the blame. Nevertheless, I have tried to stress the necessity of physically experiencing his sculptures. Walking all around one, looking at it from every possible angle, is basic and essential. After all, it is not only the control of the viewer in the 2-D/3-D pattern described above which will enhance enjoyment and understanding.

Little discussed have been the works' formal properties: colour, form, texture, and shape. Sadly, except for the case of ceramic sculpture, colour is usually seen as a superfluous or applied aspect of sculpture, an afterthought. In Pethick's case, Isaac Newton is responsible for determining his colour sense. Newton's discovery of the spectrum influenced a number of artists and theorists in succeeding centuries: M. E. Chevreul, author of *The Principles of Harmony and Contrast of Colours and Their Applications to the Arts* (1839), posited relationships between complementary hues; Georges Seurat's Divisionism and Post-Impressionism broke colour down into separate adjacent modules; and, in our own century, Josef Albers also stressed in his 1963 book, *The Interaction of Colour,* the intrinsic qualities of colours which, when placed next to one another, tended to expand or contract, advance or recede.

At first, colour does not seem a critical part of Pethick's sculptures either. The black and white colouring derived from the recycled appliances has struck some critics as icy, northern, and Canadian. The advent of the integral photos combined with the adjacent floor objects, however, reintroduced colour in a subtle, secondary way. Viewed separately, the colour photographs insure that the stereoscopic image of "material space" is in colour, like "real life". Examining the floor objects, one notes their bright industrial colour, as in *Drawbridge Dilemma* (1990), which places colour in a central role. Finally, the introduction of spectral colour with prismatic plastic taping, produced a virtual signature material for Pethick, strongly influencing his American followers like

Buster Simpson. Truly Newtonian, diffraction grating tape (as it is also known) splits up the spectrum of colour to give a rainbow effect and lends a chromatically dynamic surface depending upon the proximity of light. At the same time, strictly observable aesthetic choice seems avoided whether by the introduction of spectra–tape or in the use of found or readymade, pre–coloured objects.

Form is baroque and elusive in Pethick's work. Considering the very presence of "material space" manages to make the term seem a contradiction of terms, volume in its traditional sculptural sense does not really exist in this case. Yet again, as the recent pieces attest, form can inhabit volume and coexist with the literally intangible form of the "material space". In fact, in order to fully appreciate the complicated perceptual battlefield he sets up in each work, the bulky forms of the floor objects are absolutely essential to the success of the hovering, immaterial 3–D image. In this way, he has redefined sculptural form in the late 20th century, extrapo–lating the Futurists' notion of exploding forms into the dispersed, renewed "figure/ground" relationship in his current work.

Texture is less elusive but equally key to unravelling the appeal of Pethick's art. For a sculptor so preoccupied with the evanescent, the intangible, the purely optical, it would be easy to forego the tactile. If we disregard our plan to experience a Pethick sculpture all at once, floating image and all, it is possible to isolate the various textures he has used to strengthen the physical character and believability of the floor components: smooth, sleek, sticky, rough, and possibly wet. The use of silicon gel as a binding agent, surrogate drawing or painting element, and general fix–it material is an important part of texture in Pethick's studio

procedures. Porcelain–enamel often acts as a pristine white ground for the skeleton of a work: shiny, durable, reusable, and with hints of a previous "life" as refrigerator, washing machine, or stove. Glass also has its own changeable texture and he has employed the entire range of glass' flexible properties as texture: liquid–appearing, broken and jagged, opaque and mysterious. Other hardware–store concoctions such as tar, duct tape, rubber, and glue also lend a variety of textures which, in their generally colourless or monochromatic character, serve as foils for the rainbow hues of the spectra–tape.

Shape is the outline of form. With Pethick, the perception of shape is the dawn of vision. Just as form in his work is eccentric and baroque, so its sister, shape, mixes straight lines with curved, circles with squares. To begin with, the circular shape of the human eye and, then, the optical lens, is the leitmotif shape in his art. Repeated circles comprise the integral photo gridwork; the fly's eye lens camera he made; and the car tire or ends of the cardboard tubes in *Let Sleeping Dogs Lie* (1989). It is an elemental shape, "easier" on the eye than straight lines or spiky outlines.

Much of Pethick's attitude toward shape involves an effort to recapture basic recognizable shapes which human experience has imprinted upon our memory at an early age. The kitty; the dog; the full–figured *Replica of Willendorf* (1981–82) (as mother?), these are outlines of recognizable images accessible to all. Rather than delineating them clearly, the artist has depended upon the mind's power to identify such shapes quickly, thus using shape as a shorthand for sculptural volume or form. Taken along with colour and texture, form and shape assemble together neatly in a

Pethick sculpture after repeated viewing. In fact, dismantling them and then recomposing them in our field of vision not only describes the way we experience his sculpture; it describes how we first encounter any unfamiliar setting in the world at large.

CONCLUSION

The link between perceiving Pethick's art and how we perceive the unfamiliar world in general underscores the profundity of his achievement. His concept of "material space", which I have tried to explain and which is also expanded upon in his own accompanying artist's statement, is a combination of craftsmanship and aesthetic content. Both properties, making and meaning, are tightly though often cumbersomely connected in his art, just as the cumbersome size of the early camera was necessary to get the first ineffable, dematerialized images of the world.

The camera and the photograph, the laser and the holo–gram, all these technological developments are extensions of the human eye and brain and all have changed the nature of our vision. In so doing, as Jerry Pethick's art reminds us, they have altered the basis of our perception of the world around us.

By making us aware that "vision is not a hierarchical sense", that it is readily dependent upon how objects are presented before us, he is telling us how uncertain our optical vision is, thus undermining any smug beliefs we may hold about the world.

Therefore, such a challenging stance renders him radically subversive and significant because, once we accept his challenge about our precarious visual hold on the world, we must begin to question everything. At the same time, perhaps paradoxically, he has done this through reasserting the autonomy of the art object, a very conservative, modernist, or "post/prehistoric" (as he would say) thing to do.

Spanning ideologies, preserving one status quo (art) while demolishing another (vision), Pethick is an important artist because this is what great artists have always done: subtly question our beliefs, raise hopes about greater possibilities, and convey this challenge through the crafting of an object which offers us a new vision of an old world.

Jerry Pethick:

Armchair

Traverse,

1987.

Photograph:

Daniel Smith

In The Eyes
of
This Beholder

ANNETTE HURTIG

Overleaf: Jerry Pethick,

Semaphore Goya, *1991.*

Photo: Daniel Smith

Since at least the Renaissance, Western civilization, its History and Culture have been promulgated and imposed from a single-point perspective, from the point of view, the privileged position, of the enfranchised European heterosexual white male. The global technologies and economies of our era, which are the outcome of this single-point perspective, have been reductive, totalizing and oppressive, if only because they inscribe universalized versions of humanity, institutions and power relationships within a relentlessly material and singular and seamlessly teleologic History.

Now, even while this era's hegemony effects further fragmentation of the social realm in an ever more pervasive reign of Reason and compliance, tangibly and intangibly making reality ever more elusive and freedom ever more illusory, Jerry Pethick explores an eidetic memory of space in an other reality. In an unpublished text, "The Bases for Spatial Exploration," he recalls memories of this space from childhood:

perhaps the sandwich of air created by the two deep banks of the creek at my grandfather's, where I spent several days making the cliff dwellings of an imagined civilization take

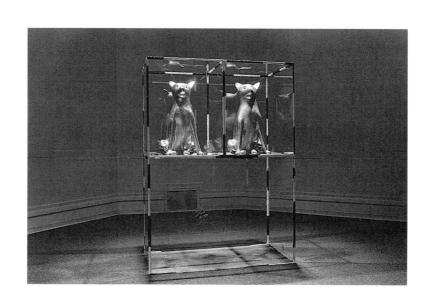

Jerry Pethick:

Installation view of

Sundogs/Actual and

Virtual, *Vancouver Art*

Gallery, 1981. Photo:

Jim Gorman

shape and become real for me; added to that, that childhood vision we experience [which] makes a location or a toy become real, and this tangible belief often commandeers, without knowing, the housing of space as well. Some of that ability to exist elsewhere disappears, but the echoes [remain] and reminders were added — by viewmasters' stereo space, 3D in various forms, and the curious experience of mining, where nothing visually exists without light, and the light describes the space that you inhabit.

Rather than replicating the space of waking reality, in *Material Space* Pethick effects the imaginary yet *real* space of daydreams wherein perception of dimension and detail is heightened, as if magnified by the mind, and time and motion are contemplative and serene. This daydream space offers and authorizes autonomous choice, subjectivity, complementarity, and intense pleasure; it seems to invite repose and reflection. For Pethick there is pleasure as well in the making and in the discovery: in the mystery, the investigation, the unravelling of clues.

I've been told that as a boy Pethick came close to losing an eye; that he held the loose eye in place with his hand as he ran to get assistance. Still attached within the socket, the one eye watched his running feet while the other looked ahead to ascertain the way. I suspect that Jerry Pethick experiences the world in some extraordinary way, in a way that puts him at odds, restless and discontent, with versions of reality that most of us accept. In his art work he visibly articulates his restlessness, his discontent, by insisting on the possibility of diverse ways of seeing, knowing and being.

His "first intrigue with light" occurred while he was working underground in the Levack hardrock nickel mine in northern Ontario. He recalls waiting for a controlled series of explosions within the mine, wearing a miner's lamp on his head and watching a transparent but visible plume of cigarette smoke ascend, fragment and shudder with each blast, and then coalesce again once the disruption was over. That momentary perception of tangible space, made visible by the smoke particles and the light and the explosive shattering of space, survives for Jerry Pethick as a memory more *real* than ordinary reality, as a paradigm, an originary experience, and as an impetus for his work.

In 1957 he left Canada to study in England. Between 1964 and 1968 he worked with salvaged transparent thermo-plastics, layering transparent and opaque materials and colour in sculptural works that explored spatial relationships. During these years in England Pethick travelled often to the European continent. In 1968 he encountered integral photography and holography and returned to North America to play a leading role in the exploration and development of holographic technology then underway in Ann Arbor, Michigan. A relatively new and cumbersome technology at that time, holography interested Pethick because it manipulated light to produce illusory space. In 1971 he co-founded the San Francisco School of Holography. The excitement of discovery he had initially experienced with holography soon waned, however, as the limitations of production and presentation in that medium became apparent. Although Pethick's interest in light, optics and the creation of illusory space continued, he left holography to investigate other options, other modes of inquiry.

His research eventually and repeatedly led him back to Paris, to a period of scientific and artistic ferment at the turn of the last century, to the work of Brancusi, Duchamp, Boccioni, Seurat and, perhaps most pertinent in the context of the current exhibition, to Gabriel Lippmann. Records of Lippmann's investigations into the principles of light interference, spectral colour as a function of light, and colour and stereo photography provided the clues which catalyzed Pethick's excitement about illusory space. Lippman had hypothesized replication of the fly's eye wherein the many single lenses within the fly's composite eye would produce single image multi-point perspective and would thus allow mobile shifting perception of an expanded three-dimensional field.

As early as 1969 Pethick was beginning to construct and experiment with integral photography, the fly's eye lens system of static image array and fresnel lens combinations that are the leitmotif in *Material Space*. Pethick's current image array installation works, which are the outcome of twenty years of inquiry into illusory space, are also evidence of this artist's determination to delimit both art and technology. Yet beyond, or perhaps beneath, the technical innovation involved in Pethick's realization of integral photography, or his delimitation of high art's material and conceptual fields of operation, Pethick's project seems to pose an urgent epistemological question, namely: could another mode of perception, the perception in motion of space as tangible dimensionality, open new ways of imagining, being, thinking and choosing?

In "The Bases for Spatial Exploration," Pethick credits Gabriel Lippmann with the technical and theoretical bases for his continuing project, and he also refers to Boccioni as an important influence:

early awakening to the effect of exterior existence, of manipulated and fashioned growth from one restless configuration to another, was greatly helped by Boccioni's vision of the seamless universe, where one could pile up in heaps musical notes and select small winds to drift through the memories structured by intent, and [where] gravity could be convinced to hold the song upside down. At last, if not [to render] part of reality for sustained examination, then, at least, to reorder the world in a personal gravity. The constant attempt to restructure in a way to be more meaningful. . .

In a catalogue essay written to accompany Pethick's *Traces Of Discovery* exhibition (1983), curator Scott Watson refers to him as an archaeologist of sorts on a rescue mission:

to recapture a moment of imaginary freedom when science was still practised by individuals and the commmerce of ideas between scientists, artists and engineers produced a vision of reality [with which] we still have not come to terms . . . . But we have lost the new consciousness and the new history, through wars, through suppression by totalitarian regimes and through the vast machinery of repression and fragmentation [by] which late capitalism's societies maintain order. . . . For Pethick history is perception.

Watson suggests that Pethick's interest in "the unexplored possibilities inherent in Boccioni's theorizing" arises from the latter's discovery of "the *drama* of the de-materialized object. . . . It is in that drama that Pethick sees the possibility for spiritual freedom and a reclamation of the imagination."

I met Jerry Pethick first in 1976 on the west coast of Canada.

At that time he was working toward completion of a series of works, which he exhibited at the Vancouver Art Gallery in 1979, entitled *The Eskimo/Kreighoff Proximity Device: A Cultural Osmosis.* In the curatorial essay published to accompany the exhibition Ted Lindberg states:

> Initially it is an ode to a mythic Canada in that Pethick applies his theories to the memory of the indigenous North American peoples, especially the Inuit, the cosmonauts of the north in their dimensionless . . . original isolation; and to Cornelius Kreighoff, selected to personify the relentless 19th century [proliferation of] European [influence] on this continent which was simultaneously liberating and destructive.

Constructed after his return to Canada from England and Europe via the United States, this series of sculptures and panels combines Pethick's renewed awareness of Canada with his experience of European civilization. The title refers to Cornelius Kreighoff, the Dutch-born and German-trained artist, who in the mid-nineteenth century travelled from Europe to North America to investigate and eventually settle in the colonies. Although he did not purport to be a scientist, as a painter Kreighoff was a trained observer; he may well have thought of his paintings as objective recordings of the terrain and the people he encountered. Kreighoff also collected botanical samples which he sold in Europe. His paintings and the botanical collections provided Europe with information about the New World, just as photography, and eventually film and video, would later provide 'empirical data.' European metaphysics no doubt coloured his vision and determined his perspective and the nature of his activities. Yet his

Jerry Pethick, The Eskimo/Krieghoff Proximity Device (Krieghoff Book), *1979.*

33

paintings were not well received in Europe; they struck his European audience as hyperbolic, bizarre, so vivid were the colours of the land, so strange the inhabitants' appearance. Thus Kreighoff was simultaneously an imposter and a puppet: an imposter in the view of the Europeans who considered his version of the colonies unbelievable, and a puppet in his perhaps unconscious yet unavoidable role as an instrument for the transference of European civilization.

Pethick's *Cultural Osmosis* takes Cornelius Kreighoff's portrayal/betrayal — his particular and historical nineteenth century position as a "stranger in a strange land" — and conflates Kreighoff with that quintessential Canadian icon, the generic, authorized and official, and hence ahistorical Eskimo. Pethick's selection of the Eskimo is overtly programmatic: it points to the other unauthorized, unofficial native "Indian" cultures which, although contiguous with virtually all Canadian settlements, have been rendered invisible, until recent uprisings, through repression, supression and oppression. In contrast, endoctrination by mythological accounts of Eskimo survival in the North enables Canadian children to respond to inquiries about Eskimos, igloos, iceflows and dogsleds.

Several works in *The Eskimo/Krieghoff Proximity Device* refer to Peter Pitseolak (1902-1973), an Inuit who took up the weapons of the enemy, including the technology of photography, in order to record his peoples' threatened and fading culture, a culture made obsolete by an encroaching and invasive single-point perspective. Like Kreighoff, Pitseolak collected and recorded, but with a different purpose. Pitseolak had no interest in objectivity or empirical evidence. He documented his own culture — its words, language, stories, artifacts — not to analyze and master, but

Jerry Pethick: The

Eskimo/Krieghoff

Proximity Device

(Pitseolak

Portrait), *1978.*

34

Jerry Pethick:

Imposter Puppet/

This is an

Investigation You

Know, (detail),

1980-1981.

in order to preserve it, at least in part, from the relentless and indomitable invasion of Western civilization and modernity. There is, of course, a certain irony in his recourse to the camera, the white man's magic box. Pethick reconstructs this device in frosty-looking etched translucent glass, and he ambiguously titles it "Ghost Camera." In this conjunction of two nouns, which is the nominative? Is the ghost within or behind the camera, or pictured by it?

The dialectics of *The Eskimo/Kreighoff Proximity Device: A Cultural Osmosis* disclose the distortions of cultural constructs inscribed from a single-point perspective. These dialectics call into question a form of consciousness, a consciousness abstracted and removed from the lived experiences of others, that would taxonomize others into extinction. Pethick therein denies the traditional Western propositions of Truth and History. For Jerry Pethick there can be no last word, no full picture. "For Pethick, history is perception." From his own acknowledged and unavoidable position as a twentieth century imposter/puppet, and in league with Kreighoff and Pitseolak, Pethick asks: "Who are these Eskimos?" and "Who was this Kreighoff?" He provides no answers, only a re-presentation of the now familiar iconography.

The intent of Pethick's queries is to free Kreighoff, Pitseolak, himself and others from identities constructed and imposed by Western patriarchy. Pethick confronts Western consciousness in an effort to overcome its conventions, to move beyond its limitations and distortions. Moreover, he refuses the traditional categories and conventions of Western aesthetics and epistemology. Re-thinking and re-imagining aesthetics and epistemology toward such delimitation requires as well a resistance to the technologies and economies of modernity. This resistance in

Pethick's work signals his determination to discover or uncover other ways of seeing, thinking, making, doing, and being. Pethick's project consists of seeing the unseeable, of extending the limits of the imaginable. Challenging us to think beyond the strictures of conventional dualities such as truth/fiction, appearance/reality, or object/subject, it provokes us to experience "beyond the confines of categories, without the mechanisms of defense such categories offer and conceal and by which they are maintained."[1]

The image array or fly's eye lens works presented in *Material Space* require time and motion. Comprised of a foregrounded three-dimensional sculptural component and a two-dimensional photographic image array mounted vertically in conjunction with a superimposed plane of finely tuned transparent fresnel lenses, they invite the viewer to enter and perambulate a sculptural surround. As the viewer approaches, the multitude of snapshots behind the lenses become discernible. As the viewer focuses on one of the photo images seen through a single lens, the picture is magnified. Moving back, away from the image array, toward the sculptural element, first two, then three images or more are optically joined to create the illusion of a three-dimensional space. The conjunction of the two vertical two-dimensional planes, image plane and lens plane, creates the illusion of an expanded, slightly fuzzy, low resolution, daydream-like space. Each viewer perceives the space differently, from a particular position according to their vantage point, as it is determined by their height and the particular physiology of their eyes. And each controls, or chooses, where the images begin to be apprehended, where they gel, coalesce, expand and disappear. The effect is like a chimera, illusory, intangible, and yet it is retrievable at will.

Pethick thinks of his *oeuvre* as an attempt to realize or

materialize expanded sculptural space: that is, the space not inhabited but rather constituted by the sculptural object in its surround. He experiences this space of the sculptural surround as a positive, material, active, tangible, implicit and necessary aspect of sculpture. He speaks about his quest for the realization of this illusory space as if it is a search for some kind of holy grail.

Pethick works with static forms that contain, occupy and implicate space. He shuffles between these two and three-dimensional static forms. His most recent work, the fly's eye image array series, invites the viewer to replicate or re-invent his dance, a choreography which resembles the movements of a painter painting: moving forward and back to refocus, tuning the image. Moving around and between the constituent parts of these works, occupying and perambulating the site, the viewer moves through several points of view, apprehends a multiplicity of objects and images, and, in the reading of clues and the discovery of relative positions in space and moments in time, experiences a kind of visual discourse upon material space — a reality, constituted of objects and space made material, material and everyday, which is tangible, and nonetheless a constructed illusion.

Because ours is a time of expanding and insidious domination, domination so pervasive and insidious that we often accept it as in our interest, as legitimate and beneficent, reality itself has become illusory. Pleasure is determined, desire is prescribed. When a sanitized simulation such as the Gulf Crisis — a spectacle of displayed and hidden powers played out on an information table convened by those who purport to be experts and constructed without bodies, blood, or death — is made available for viewing at prime time on televisions in homes around the globe and it is presented as a play of righteous power that would have us believe that there can be a surgically clean, bloodless, deathless, technological war of collateral damage and smart missiles, then disaster is triumphant.[2] When simulation supercedes reality, then is seeing still believing? Perhaps because I am suspect of such illusions, I initially had difficulty understanding Pethick's urgency and his obvious pleasure in and excitement about his quest for illusory space. Like other readers of cultural theorists such as Guy Debord and Jean Baudrillard, I associate illusion with spectacle and simulation; and these I recognize as modes of deception and domination, means to quell dissent.[3] Yet, if we are to re-imagine our world as a place without dominance and oppression, without "disaster triumphant," will we not need to imagine new ways of seeing, new ways of thinking and being? To do so we will need to resist rather than comply, and thus, also, to question traditional Western metaphysics, even if only momentarily. Might it be in an eidetic and now vestigal memory of reality, in the imaginary, in the daydream, that we may discover ways to resist the difficulties of expression, of experience, of thought, "as these are inseparable from truth and history, constructed, known and unknown, in the present, a present in which a past and a future are always at stake"?[4]

Undoubtedly Pethick's work might be read as a kind of traditional male exploration of technical limits. Yet even his approach to technical problems is unorthodox. Rather than complex and mystifying mechanisms, he invents simple, eco-nomical solutions. These he leaves visible, as clues, and as evidence of his process. Although I am no technical expert, I recognize this work's ingenuity, its austere economy and its audacity, its refusal of conventions and polemics in favour of the disclosure of an inquiry. Pethick's work — work in both senses of that word, the product and the process — seems alive, always changing, never at rest, always questioning. And it enlivens me: I become aware of myself in space and time and motion. I take pleasure in this seeing and believing as an autonomous cognizant subject. And, I associate what I imagine to be Pethick's refusal of prescribed conventions with my own struggles and resistance.

Speaking in *Cassandra* about writing as one form of resistance, Christa Wolf asserts the importance of such provocation: "I think it is important to articulate positions of resistance. . . . It cannot be wrong, I think, for literature to always provoke the moral and aesthetic standards of its own culture or civilization a little. Moreoever, this is something that fosters peace." Michel Foucault, in his investigations of Western cultural, political and scientific technologies, identifies resistance as perhaps the most potent avenue of pleasure that remains available to us. Foucault goes so far as to suggest that at times silence, the refusal to articulate a position, may be the only and unavoidable response, the most potent form of resistance.

Rather than articulating theoretical or ideological arguments, Pethick's work evinces day-to-day strategies for existing, and for resisting an oppressive global hegemony operating through immense systems, systems that entail ownership of, access to and control over information, mobility and space. The contemporary erosion of space, the disappearance of space as a place to play and to imagine, signals a purposeful circumscription of freedom. Jerry Pethick wishes to delimit space: to make material and visible space to move, to experiment, to seek understanding, to query. Pethick seeks to make a space free of requisite compliance, free of domination. Space to question and thus to speak or remain silent. Space to choose.

Jerry Pethick investigates the quotidian: space, motion, time and the mechanics of scopic perception. He uses simple mechanisms, few tools, familiar materials. Yet his effect is disruptive of the *status quo*. Disturbed by the Western reality model with its unrelenting inscription, prescription and circumscription, he seeks to dematerialize History, to rupture the dominance and oppression of instrumental Reason, to fracture and disperse Truth, to query and defy stasis, and to expose and thus demystify the technologies of simulation.

From a Pethick point of view there is no single Truth or History: truth and history are polylogic and multivalent. No longer absolute entities, they proliferate, become plural, diverse and fluctuating. Pethick's truths are perceived in motion, by a body literally moving through space. Also, there is the effect of parallax, the reversal of clues and the apparent displacement of an object or an 'objective reality' or a Truth, due to perception in motion. Understanding occurs over time. And in space. Truths and realities are composed by subjective cumulative memory, through time and unfolding space, and are inflected by the pain of oppression and the pleasures of resistance and of discovery. Change, through discovery, constitutes a matrix of pleasures; stasis is pain. Pethick's remove from modernism can be understood as an abhorence of the totalizing and static. He also refuses modernity's proclivities for utopian ideologies and their reifications. Mistrust of high technology's mystifications determines his denial of all sorts of "complicated vehicles." Technologically complex presentations and representations are eschewed in favour of "simple vision . . . [as] a way of being able to select a personalized vision [version] of otherwhere, or a synthesis of the present reality, squeezing it into another portrayal or betrayal. Rejection of *status quo* systems allows a space to play in the residue."[5] Pethick's radicality within contemporary art and life generates from his unorthodox tolerance for, and pleasure in, inconstancy.

His work, concerned with making space for query, choice and silence, raises questions about authenticity, simulation, knowledge and power, for example, similar to those voiced by such theorists as Christa Wolf, Theodor Adorno, Maurice Blanchot, Jean Baudrillard and Michel Foucault. His is a project arising out of profound restlessness and discontent, sustained through more than twenty working and questioning years, aimed at the demystification of Western thought and its technologies of art, science and politics, in an attempt to disclose the false consciousness central to these modes of knowledge, revealing them to be forms of domination and oppression: forms of unseeing, "forms of unfreedom."[6]

Notes

1. I am indebted here and elsewhere in this text to Paul Kelley's insightful and unpublished essay "The Provocation of Cassandra" in which Kelley responds to Christa Wolf's writings on the myth of Cassandra.

2. My use of the phrase "disaster is triumphant" plays on a similar usage in Susan Lord's essay "Outliving Apollo's Kiss"wherein Lord's re-reading of the myth of Cassandra refers similarly to the Gulf Crisis. Lord's essay was published by the Fine Art Gallery, University of British Columbia, Vancouver, to accompany an exhibition by Cornelia Wyngaarden. The notion that the history of Western civilization "radiates disaster triumphant" must be credited to Max Horkheimer and Theodor Adorno, *Dialectic of Enlightenment*, trans. John Cumming (New York: Continum, 1972), p. 3f.

3. See, for example, Jean Baudrillard's *Simulations* and Guy Debord's *Society of the Spectacle.*

4. Paul Kelley, Op. Cit.

5. Jerry Pethick, in a letter from the artist dated July 11, 1991.

6. Paul Kelley, Op. Cit.

Material Space

BY: **JERRY PETHICK**

My current work relates aspects of volume and image of deep illusory space, created by integral photography, to the presence of tangible sculptural elements. These elements stand free and exist in proximity to the volume of space inherent within the fly's eye lens photo array. With this dimensional imaging technique, the spatial reconstruction is usually inversed back to front, the composite whole hard to hold within one's perception. I correct this somewhat, by altering the order of the photographic record. This manipulation still gives some reverse parallax, but the sensually created volume exists through corrections the brain automatically makes as it adjusts the single composite image to a point of acceptance. The solid–looking space created by this illusory system exists in rapport with the real density of actual material and form of the sculptural elements. The optically tangible volume apparent here encapsulates the space and represents it as an object and spatial vista.

The glimpsed space interacts sensually and the low resolution image is a perception that verifies the sense of material space.

The free dimensional nature of the array, made by the many photos from different points of view, helps the related interaction between the sculptural elements and the single composite reconstruction. Essence of tactile material, juxtaposed with tangible space, re-evaluates the hierarchy that traditionally made material substance the predominant entity of sculptural expression. The illusory space created by this integrated imaging technique gives perceptual volume a presence of its own, malleable and usable as other tangible material, an equal in the democratic use of material.

Cable Street Studios,
London [UK],
October 28, 1990

WORKS IN THE EXHIBITION

(all works are collection of the artist)

Waterworks Park, 1972
280 x 215 cm
plastic, silicone, steel, dye, fresnel lenses

Armchair Traverse, 1987
90 x 120 x 20 cm
mixed media / photo array
glass, aluminum, silicone, duratran lights, plastic
fresnel lenses

Colossus of Kindergarten, 1987/89
300 x 360 x 330 cm
mixed media
records, spectrafoil, blanket, aluminum, glass,
silicone, wooden boat, bicycle tire, stone, lead,
lights

Bobsled, 1989
150 x 150 cm
mill paper, graphite

Drawing on the Street of Dreams, 1989/91
300 x 520 x 450 cm
mixed media / photo array
aluminum, cable wire, wood, fresnel lenses,
photographs, plywood, blankets, bottles, stainless
steel, enamelled steel, cork, wire, stool

Plummet, 1989/91
260 x 190 x 40 cm
aluminum, paper
handmade grey embossed paper, graphite and
aluminum shape

Composite Portrait, 1990

233 x 249 x 33 cm

mixed media / photo array

wood, glass, clear and red fresnel plastic lenses, plastic clock, stainless steel, Carborundum, license plates, graphite, photographs, drawings, enamelled steel, aluminum, bowling ball

Semaphore Goya, 1991

300 x 450 x 600 cms

mixed media / photo array

photographs, fresnel lenses, stones, wood, steel, wire, stainless steel, glass, lights, plastic, mirror, coal, blown glass, aluminum silicone

Snake Deletion, Haystack and Sunrise, 1991

260 x 900 x 450 cms

mixed media / photo array

blown glass, carpet, sulphur, patio bricks, stones, Verticell cardboard, lights, photographs, fresnel lenses, glass

Jerry Pethick: Composite Portrait, *1990.*

J E R R Y   P E T H I C K

Selected Solo Exhibitions

1991   *Material Space*, Southern Alberta Art Gallery, Lethbridge, Alberta

1989   *Recent Sculpture*, Cliff Michel Gallery, Seattle, Washington [USA]

1988   Grace Gallery, Vancouver, British Columbia

1986   *Le Dot/Transition in Progress*, 49th Parallel, Centre for Contemporary
Canadian Art, New York, New York [USA]

1985   *Le Dot/Transition in Progress*, Galerie Crousel Robelin BAMA, Paris [France]

1984   *Traces of Discovery*, Vancouver Art Gallery, Vancouver

1983   *Traces of Discovery*, Canadian Cultural Centre, Paris [France]

1982   *Approaches*, Stones Gallery, Victoria, British Columbia

1981   *Strategems of Distortion/Sensations of Illusion: Phase 2, and/or*, Seattle,
Washington [U.S.A.]

        Strategems of Distortion/Sensations of Illusion: Phase 1, Malaspina Gallery,
Nanaimo, British Columbia

1979   *The Eskimo/Krieghoff Proximity Device: A Cultural Osmosis*, Vancouver Art
Gallery, Vancouver

1975   *Look-Out*, F.A.D. Gallery, Wolverhampton, Midlands [UK]

1973   *Lighthouse*, Fine Arts Gallery, University of British Columbia, Vancouver

1972   *Space Array*, NOVA 1 Gallery, Berkeley, California [USA]

1970   *Drawings*, 20/20 Gallery, London, Ontario

Selected Group Exhibitions

1991   Galerie Brenda Wallace, Montreal, Quebec

       Cliff Michel Gallery, Seattle, Washington [USA]

1990   *Arbora Versa*, Contemporary Art Gallery, Vancouver

1989   *Canadian Biennial of Contemporary Art*, National Gallery of Canada, Ottawa

1986   *Focus: Kanadische Kunst von 1960-1985*, 20th International Art Market, Cologne [Germany]

       Vancouver Now/Vancouver '86 Insertion, Walter Phillips Gallery, The Banff Centre, Banff, Alberta (national tour)

       Making History, Vancouver Art Gallery, Vancouver

1984   *Reconstituted Elements*, Open Space, Victoria, British Columbia

1982   *Mise en Scene: Kim Adams, Mowry Baden, Roland Brener, Al McWilliams, Liz Magor, Jerry Pethick*, Vancouver Art Gallery, Vancouver

1970   *N Dimensional Space*, Finch College Museum of Art—Contemporary Wing, New York, New York [USA]

1969   *Holography*, Cranbrook Academy of Art, Bloomfield Hills, Michigan [USA]

1968   *Ed Pickett and Jerry Pethick*, Fulham Palace Studios, London [UK]

1967   John Moore Memorial Exhibition, Walker Art Gallery, Liverpool [UK]

1965   *Six Canadian Artists*, South London Gallery, London [UK]

1964   *Young Commonwealth Artists 1964*, Whitechapel Gallery, London [UK]

1958   *Young Contemporaries*, RBA Galleries, London [UK]

Awards

Canada Council A Grant, 1984, 1990
Canada Council Arts Bursary, 1967, 1968
Purchase award, Arts Council of Great Britain, 1968
London [UK] county council education grant, 1961-64

Selected Public Collections

Canada Council Art Bank, Ottawa
Art Gallery of Ontario, Toronto
Arts Council of Great Britain, London [UK]
Bibliothèque Nationale, Paris [France]
Metropolitan Art Museum, Amsterdam [Netherlands]
City Light 1% for Art, Portable Works Collection, Seattle Arts Commission,
Seattle, Washington [USA]
Vancouver Art Gallery

Selected Bibliography

Annette Hurtig and Matthew Kangas, *Jerry Pethick/Material Space.* Lethbridge,
        Alberta: Southern Alberta Art Gallery, 1991, illus.
Mark Frutkin, "Highlight: Canadian Biennial", *Ottawa Magazine,* October, 1989.
Ron Glowen, "Jerry Pethick: Sculptural Works", *Artweek,* November 30, 1989, illus.
Annette Hurtig, *Island Influence.* Hornby Island, B.C.: Hornby Festival Society, 1989.

Bill Little, "Voluminous Luminosity: Some Scents of Jerry Pethick's Work", *Capilano Review,* Fall, 1989, illus.

Diana Nemiroff, *Canadian Biennial of Contemporary Art.* Ottawa: National Gallery of Canada, 1989, illus.

Stephen Godfrey, "Exhibitions showcase three distinctive B.C. artists", *The Globe and Mail,* March 12, 1988.

Elizabeth Godley, "This intellectual art will have you seeking clues", *The Vancouver Sun,* February 22, 1988.

Art Perry, "Pethick's Fun House"*, The Province,* March 1, 1988, illus.

Jean-Marc Boileau, "Six galeries recoivent Vancouver à Montréal", *Journal Liaison St-Louis*, January 21, 1987.

Jocelyne LePage, "Arts et spectacles", *La Presse, Montreal,* January 17, 1987.

Shirley Madill, "Vancouver Now/Vancouver '86: Insertion", *The VAG* [Vancouver Art Gallery] *Magazine,* February/March, 1987.

Manon Blanchette, *Vancouver Now/Vancouver '86 Insertion.* Banff, Alberta: Walter Phillips Gallery, The Banff Centre, 1986.

Judy Williams, *Jerry Pethick: Le Dot/Transition in Progress.* New York: 49th Parallel, Centre for Contemporary Canadian Art, 1986, illus.

Robert Amos, "Art: A delightful alchemy of light", *Monday Magazine,* February 24-March 1, 1984.

Robert Amos, "Art: Some parting thoughts", *Monday Magazine,* March 16-22, 1984.

[Anon.], "Les jeux de lumière de Jerry Pethick", *Canada Today/Canada Aujourd'hui,* January, 1984.

James O. Caswell, "Letters: Review a dismal example of low state of art criticism", *The Vancouver Sun,* May 28, 1984.

Regina Hackett, "B. C. Exhibit: Pethick at his best", *Seattle Post-Intelligencer,* March 5, 1984.

Eve Johnson, "Art in history's grip", *The Vancouver Sun,* March 14, 1984.

Matthew Kangas, "Jerry Pethick and Buster Simpson: Comparative Subversions", unpublished lecture delivered at "A symposium on the work of Jerry Pethick, Sculptor", Department of Fine Arts, University of British Columbia, Vancouver, B.C., March 31, 1984.

John Bentley Mays, "Enigmatic sculpture in twilight of dream", *The Globe and Mail,*
May 31, 1984.

Scott Watson, "Terminal City: Place, Culture, and the Regional Inflection", *Vancouver:
Art and Artists 1931-1983.* Vancouver: Vancouver Art Gallery, 1983, illus.

Scott Watson, "Boccioni's smile: Jerry Pethick's Traces of Discovery", *Jerry Pethick:
Traces of Discovery—Seurat/Lippman/1901 Air Show.* Vancouver: Vancouver Art
Gallery, 1984, illus.

Joyce Woods, "Visual Arts", *Georgia Straight,* March 2-9, 1984.

[Anon.], "Vu à Paris: Jeux de lumière et scultures récents: Jerry Pethick expose", *Le
Rouergue,* October 8, 1983.

Scott Watson, *Jerry Pethick.* Paris: Canadian Cultural Centre, 1983, illus.

Robert Amos, "From Holograms to the Hornby Island Dump", *Monday Magazine,* June
18-24, 1982, illus.

Regina Hackett, review, *Seattle Post-Intelligencer,* May 15, 1982.

Susan Mertens, "Not an exhibition for wandering minds", *The Vancouver Sun,* May 12,
1982.

Greg Snider, "Mise en scène: The Vancouver Art Gallery", *Parachute,* September/
October/November, 1982, illus.

David Watmough, "Show by young B. C. sculptors recalls memories of yesteryear",
The Province, June 17, 1982.

Scott Watson, "Strategems of Distortion: An interview with Jerry Pethick", in *Mise en
Scène: Kim Adams, Mowry Baden, Roland Brener, Al McWilliams, Liz Magor, Jerry
Pethick.* Vancouver: Vancouver Art Gallery, 1982, illus.

Jane Young, "Mise en scène: Jerry Pethick", *Vanguard,* September, 1982, illus.

[Anon.], "Reflecting works", *Nanaimo Daily Free Press,* February 5, 1981, illus.

Regina Hackett, "Life Fractured in a Folky Way", *Seattle Post-Intelligencer,* April 2,
1981, illus.

Jeff Berner, *The Holography Book.* New York: Avon Books, 1980.

Robert Amos, "Jerry Pethick", *Artswest,* September/October, 1979, illus.

Ted Lindberg, "Introduction" to *Jerry Pethick: The Eskimo/Krieghoff Proximity Device: A
Cultural Osmosis.* Vancouver: Vancouver Art Gallery, 1979, illus., with
spectratape appliqué.

Ted Lindberg, "The Eskimo/Krieghoff Proximity Device/Jerry Pethick", *Vanguard,*
August, 1979, illus.

Isabel Partridge, "Artist depicts Inuit energy", *Summer Savant,* June 1, 1979, illus.

Marc R. D'Alleyrand, "Holograms: Putting the Third D Into the Catalog", *Wilson Library Bulletin,* May, 1977, illus.

Douglas Davis, "Art: The Nth Dimension", *Newsweek,* June 15, 1970.

Ted McBurnett and Elayne H. Varian, *N Dimensional Space.* New York: Finch College Museum of Art—Contemporary Wing, 1970, illus.

Fred Unterseher, *Holography Handbook.* New York: Museum of Holography, 1968

John Moore Memorial Exhibition. Liverpool [UK]: Walker Art Gallery, 1967.

Six Canadian Artists. London [UK]: South London Gallery, 1965.

Young Commonwealth Artists 1964. London [UK]: Whitechapel Gallery, 1964.

Writings by Jerry Pethick

Jerry Pethick, "Material Space", in Annette Hurtig and Matthew Kangas, *Jerry Pethick: Material Space.* Lethbridge, Alberta: Southern Alberta Art Gallery, 1991, illus.

Jerry Pethick, "Vision in the Blood", *Capilano Review,* Fall, 1989, p. 97, illus.

Jerry Pethick, *Le Dot/Transition in Progress.* Artist's book, 57 pp., offset-printed with spectratape appliqué. Vancouver: Privately published, 1986.

Jerry Pethick, "The Personal Domain", unpublished lecture delivered at "A symposium on the work of Jerry Pethick, Sculptor", Department of Fine Arts, University of British Columbia, March 31, 1984.

Jerry Pethick, "A Talk with Scott Watson and Stereo Interview", in *Mise en Scène: Kim Adams, Roland Brener, Al McWilliams, Liz Magor, Jerry Pethick.* Vancouver: Vancouver Art Gallery, 1982, illus.

Jerry Pethick, "Optics of Insight", in Jeff Berner, *The Holography Book.* New York: Avon Books, 1980, pp. 89-91.

Jerry Pethick, exhibition statement in the form of an excerpt from a letter to Norie Sato, in *Jerry Pethick/The Polarity Strategem/Evolved Distortion.* Seattle, Washington [USA]: *and/or,* 1981. Checklist with additional excerpt from "Bias Arrays, Un Procès sans cesse" (*Vanguard,* December 1976/January 1977)

Jerry Pethick, "Nature and Space", unpublished artist's statement, typewritten and photocopied, June 12, 1977

Jerry Pethick, "Bias arrays: A Spatial Exploration of Ideas and Concepts in Six
Lectures," unpublished outline for six artist's statements: Concepts and Image
of Spatial Thought; Documenting Consciousness; Facets of Evolving Struc-
ture; Residue of Perception; Technology Fragments; Time Tools, Hand and
Eye.Vancouver, Spring 1977.

Jerry Pethick, "Bias arrays, Un procès sans cesse", part of "Crosscurrents: Disparate
Notions and Critical Ambuscades", sponsored by The Canada Council,
Vanguard, December 1976/January 1977.

Jerry Pethick, *Light Recordings—a 3M Colour Process Book.* Artist's Book. San Francisco:
Privately published, 1974.

Jerry Pethick, *On Holography and a Way to Make Holograms.* Burlington, Ont.:
Belltower Enterprises "published in cooperation with the Umbra Foundation",
1971.

Jerry Pethick, "Statement: On Sculpture and Laser Holography", *Artscanada*, December, 1968, pp. 70-71, illus.

Overleaf:

Jerry Pethick:

Colossus of

Kindergarten,

1987-1989.

Photograph:

Daniel Smith

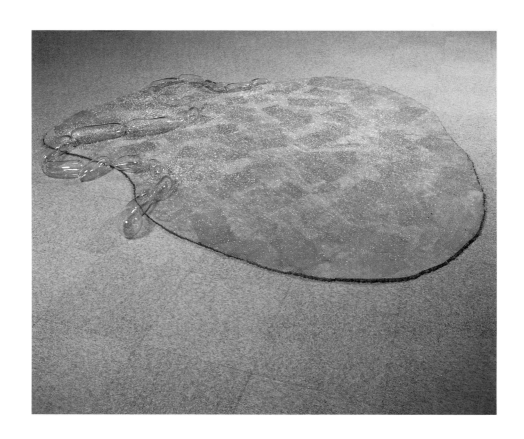

Jerry Pethick: Snake Deletion, Haystack and Sunrise (detail)*, 1991. Photograph: Daniel Smith*

존경하는 나의 어머니께
그리고 내 아이들의 멋진 엄마, 나의 아내에게

글을 쓰고 그림을 그린 **앤서니 브라운**은 1946년 영국에서 태어났습니다. 독특하고 뛰어난 작품으로 높은 평가를 받고 있는 그림책 작가 중의 한 사람으로, 많은 작품들이 전 세계에서 출간되어 널리 사랑 받고 있습니다. 1983년 〈고릴라〉로 '케이트 그린어웨이 상'과 '커트 매쉴러 상'을 받았고, 〈동물원〉으로 두 번째 '케이트 그린어웨이 상'을 받았습니다. 2000년에는 세계에서 가장 뛰어난 그림책 작가에게 주는 '한스 크리스찬 안데르센 상'을 받았습니다. 국내에 출간된 책으로는 〈미술관에 간 윌리〉〈돼지책〉〈앤서니 브라운의 행복한 미술관〉 등이 있습니다.

글을 옮긴 **허은미**는 1964년에 태어났습니다. 출판사에서 일을 하다가 지금은 어린이 책을 기획하고 글을 쓰고 있습니다. 그동안 쓴 책으로 〈종알종알 말놀이 그림책〉〈잠들 때 하나씩 들려주는 이야기〉〈똥은 참 대단해〉〈우리 몸의 구멍〉 등이 있고, 옮긴 책으로는 〈돼지책〉〈윌리와 악당 벌렁코〉〈꿈꾸는 윌리〉 등이 있습니다. 앤서니 브라운의 작품을 좋아해서, 언젠가 그에 대한 본격적인 작품론을 쓰는 게 꿈이라고 합니다.

웅진주니어

우리 엄마

초판 1쇄 발행 2005년 3월 20일 | 초판 16쇄 발행 2008년 1월 4일
글 그림 앤서니 브라운 | 옮김 허은미 | 발행인 최봉수 | 본부장 이미혜
편집장 이원주 | 편집 김혜진 | 디자인 이민옥 | 마케팅 조민호, 이현은, 박광운 | 제작 한동수, 류정옥
임프린트 웅진주니어 | 주소 서울시 종로구 동숭동 199-16 웅진빌딩 2층 | 주문전화 02-3670-1050, 팩스 02-747-1239
문의전화 02-3670-1556 | 홈페이지 http://www.wjjunior.com
발행처 (주)웅진씽크빅 | 출판신고 1980년 3월 29일 제 406-2007-00046호
한국어판 출판권 ⓒ 웅진씽크빅, 2005 | ISBN 978-89-01-04790-4 · 978-89-01-02697-8(세트)
MY MUM by Anthony Browne | Copyright ⓒ A. E .T. Browne, 2005
All rights reserved. | Korean Translation copyright ⓒ Woongjin Thinkbig Co., Ltd. 2005
This Korean edition was published by arrangement with Random House Children's Books,
London, UK through Eric Yang Agency, Seoul, KOREA.
웅진주니어는 (주)웅진씽크빅의 출판부문 임프린트사업니다.
이 책의 한국어판 출판권은 에릭양 에이전시를 통해
Random House Children's Books사와 맺은 독점계약으로 (주)웅진씽크빅에 있습니다.
저작권법에 따라 국내에서 보호받는 저작물이므로 무단전재와 복제를 금지하며,
이 책 내용의 전부 또는 일부를 이용하려면 반드시 저작권자와 (주)웅진씽크빅의 서면 동의를 받아야 합니다.
이 도서의 국립중앙도서관 출판시도서목록(CIP)은 e-CIP 홈페이지(http://www.nl.go.kr/cip.php)에서 이용하실 수 있습니다.
(CIP제어번호: CIP2004002296)

우리 엄마

글·그림 앤서니 브라운 옮긴이 허은미

웅진주니어

우리 엄마는 참 멋져요.

우리 엄마는 굉장한 요리사이고,

놀라운 재주꾼이에요.

우리 엄마는 훌륭한 화가이고,

세상에서 가장 힘이 센 여자죠!

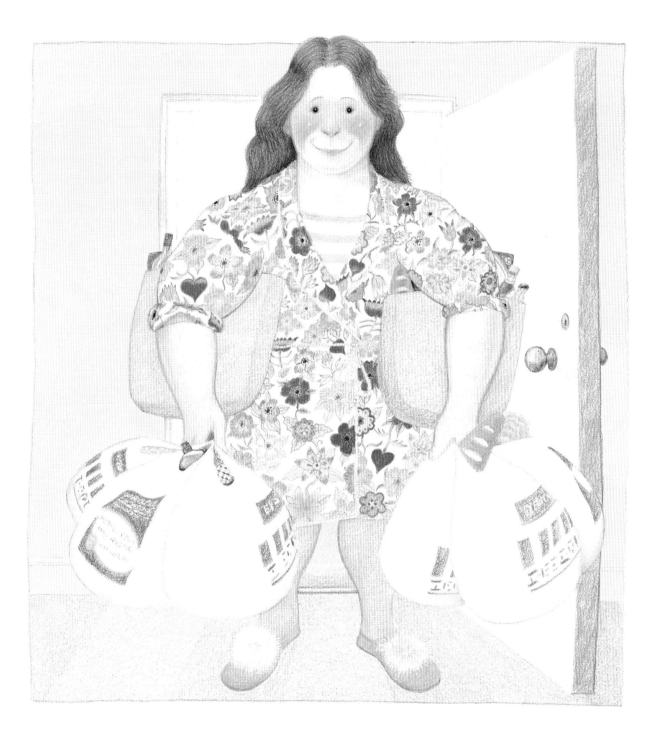

정말 멋진 우리 엄마.

우리 엄마는 마법의 정원사.
무엇이든 자라게 할 수 있어요.

그리고 우리 엄마는 착한 요정.
내가 슬플 때면 나를 기쁘게 할 수 있죠.

우리 엄마는 천사처럼 노래할 수도 있고,

사자처럼 으르릉 소리칠 수도 있어요.

정말 **정말** 멋진 우리 엄마.

우리 엄마는 나비처럼 아름답고,

안락의자처럼
편안해요.

아기 고양이처럼 부드럽고,

코뿔소처럼 튼튼해요.

정말 **정말 정말** 멋진 우리 엄마.

우리 엄마는 무용가가 되거나

우주 비행사가 될 수도 있었어요.

어쩌면 영화배우나

사장이 될 수도 있었고요.
하지만 **우리 엄마**가 되었죠.

우리 엄마는 슈퍼엄마!

나를 자주 웃게 해요. 아주 많이.

나는 엄마를 사랑해요.

그리고……

엄마도 나를 사랑한답니다!

(언제까지나 영원히…….)